Sounding the Silence

Sounding the Silence

John Skinner

LTP

LITURGY
TRAINING
PUBLICATIONS

First published in 2004 by

Gracewing Publishing
2 Southern Avenue
Leominster
Herefordshire HR6 0QF
England

SOUNDING THE SILENCE © 2005 Archdiocese of Chicago: Liturgy Training Publications, 1800 North Hermitage Avenue, Chicago IL 60622-1101; 1-800-933-1800, fax 1-800-933-7094, e-mail orders@ltp.org. All rights reserved. See our website at www.ltp.org.

Printed in the United States of America.

Library of Congress Control Number: 2005922226

ISBN 1-56854-565-7

SSIL

For Judith

*Who walks with me
in the Silence
and has helped offer it
to many another*

Table of contents

Prologue

by a Carthusian

Echoes of Silence

Various writings in this book are but sparks spiralling off from a center of fires that cannot itself be directly described. Silence is like God. The God you can say is not God.

The silence you can utter is not Silence itself. Silence is, perhaps, a direct perception of mystery, a sort of experience of the immense reality that enfolds and engenders us. For we too are part of it: we too are mystery, opening onto unlimited horizons.

This is not the reserve of the exotic mystical, it is present in each one of us, there, founding all our particular perceptions and understandings of things and of people, yet itself impossible of conceptual expression.

The Unborn cannot be conceived. He stands at the door and knocks. We let Him in when we enter quietly into ourselves to open our hearts and minds to what is beyond our little objectified, constructed world, and ego. When we have to receive what *is,* without trying to grasp it, to be in trust that all is gift and, finally, love.

Silence becomes the fullness of our fragmented words, an act of hope and faith that, beyond time and death, sin and suffering, all will be well, for all is well.

God, in himself and we and all things in Him, is love.

So here is an invitation throughout the coming year to take a moment from time to time to breathe, to live His presence in conscious awareness.

Parkminster

Prayer—a way of life

I have always held that prayer is important. But, over the past five years, my conviction has grown so that now I hold prayer to be the most important human activity that can engage us. It began when my London publisher asked me for a book about monks. There had been a best-seller that lifted the veil on nuns—why they had chosen their calling, what their lives were like. Why not ask similar questions about what makes a monk?

I had always wanted to meet the Carthusians, an elite order of hermit monks whose tradition runs back 900 years. Their life is entirely given to prayer. Unlike the Cistercians who are farmers, or the Benedictines who sometimes run schools or even parishes, these men have no set work. Their daily routine is austere, mostly spent alone in the cell and in silence. No surprise, then, that throughout the world they number less than 500 men. There is only one Charterhouse (as they call their monasteries) in the whole of the United States and a single one in England.

Parkminster, as the English Charterhouse is called, is set in a remote part of Sussex on the Southern coastline.

I was fortunate enough to persuade the Prior to allow me to spend two weeks with them, absorbing their ways, following the same routine as any novice monk. And living among them, I learned how prayer is their way of life.

This small band of hermit monks drew me into their community and for a brief but heady period, I became one of them. I rose at midnight and joined their prayer of Matins and Lauds—a stint of some three hours' chanting the psalms in Latin, listening to readings from scripture and the so-called Fathers of the Church—teachers and writers from long ago. Early the same morning, I attended their community Mass, a large part prayed in drenching silence. We worked together and I shared their vegetarian regime of one full meal each day, no breakfast and only a small supper.

All this to a purpose: I wrote a book based upon the experience entitled *Hear our Silence.* So far so good. But the Carthusians had gotten under my skin. In particular, their silent prayer began to haunt me. My wife and I decided to pray together each day for half an hour in silence. Next, a friend joined us and so we decided to go public.

I returned to the Carthusian monastery at Parkminster and confessed to the Prior, Dom Cyril, that I intended to steal their silence and offer it abroad. His reaction was instantaneous: "use our name," he declared.

Together, we developed a simple model of praying that was inviting and felt safe; although Christian in inspiration, we determined to be totally inclusive. Anyone can pray: no prayer is the same. There are no techniques, rules, or strictures—just the silent half hour for each individual to fill as they please.

For some time now, we have offered workshops on the prayer of silence; either for a day or over the weekend. A dozen or so people show up each time and from these exploratory and feeding encounters house groups have begun to sprout. Our own front door is open once a week on a Wednesday evening when people come to share the silent half hour.

Many people who have attended our prayer workshops have wanted to stay in touch. So each month I send out a letter to over a hundred "Friends of *Hear our Silence*" enclosing four weekly readings together with some thoughts to thread a theme. These readings have been well received, and from them springs this book.

Although our prayer is silent, receptive and removed from ruminative Ignatian meditation, a reading is always offered as a bridge into the silence. Perhaps a single phrase may prove useful, or a theme provide a platform. Or the reading may simply be left behind as the silent encounter unfolds.

I have used our readings over the past year to set down some of the key ideas on prayer that we meet again and again in our workshops. Essentially prayer is very simple. We come to the silence in order to find our deeper self and hope to encounter our Maker in this mysterious frontier which is the Source of Life and Love.

There can be few words, no bargains to be struck, any dialogue soon dries: the key is encounter—with myself, with the Other. As Dom Cyril says, keep it simple, there are no rules, all is gift, a fresh start to each new prayer.

Although for me personally, it is Christ who is the mainspring of my prayer, I conceive this Silence to be common to us all. For the universal language of mankind is our very being: to sound the Silence at the center of our day-to-day existence is to seek to be fully alive. And I cannot doubt that everyone I meet has not at some time reflected upon this Mystery at the heart of our world. All human experience is one. We seek this unity in loving relationships grounded in our own inner reality—our given existence received in love from the Other.

I have just begun taking the *Hear our Silence* program for silent prayer into our local prison. A dozen or so men join me on a Monday morning for a silent half hour. They welcome the silence, for prison is a noisy place; above all, they recognize the importance of attending (perhaps for the first time of noticing it) to their inner world in peace and joy. As the weeks go by, I can see how they grow both as individuals and as a group. In their praying they find healing and hope. Not for any future outcome; they have learned to pray in the *now*, to savor this moment of this particular day. The past is closed, the future yet to come. It is now that we share this precious and mysterious encounter— our deepest self and the Unnameable Other, our Maker, Keeper, Lover.

John Skinner
Axminster

first principles

No one can teach you to pray. And there are no rules as such: but wisdom indicates a few first principles to be aware of. As Ignatius of Antioch said long ago— "there is but a single Master," and he teaches us within. There is only one way to learn to pray: by praying.

So is it simply "in at the deep end"? Almost, but there are four simple first principles which will not exactly get us off to a flying start, but at least they may help us remain permanently grounded. And these are best kept in mind every time we pray until they become second nature.

We need to remember that we humans are a wonderful balance, sometimes imbalance, of spirit/mind/Self/soul and animal body, with all its senses, appetites, and energy. We must respect all these aspects as we come to pray. Now since the body is to be at rest when we pray, it is good to tune into a state of **physical quiet** before we attend to prayer. You might try simply sitting in a relaxed way, but alert and then attend to regular breathing, just for a few minutes, in and out, aware of your lungs working well and freely.

Or, you may experiment with simply walking, gently and slowly, again breathing deeply and letting any thinking process slip away. Eyes down, not attending to anything in particular, letting go of the physical. Allowing your body to calm itself and slow right down.

Second, decide your choice of **posture.** The simplest and most obvious is sitting down. But don't flop back into the best chair in the house! Chose a seat that will support you comfortably but where you will remain alert. We are trying to hold the body still and contain any protesting while the inner world is free to explore and be explored.

I don't recommend kneeling, although some favor those kneeling/meditation stools which support the body in a collapsed kneeling posture.

Some prefer to sit cross-legged, and this is very comfortable but sitting on a cushion is a good option—simply to tilt the weight forward slightly, and allow the back to remain straight. Hands resting on knees.

Having settled into your preferred position, and you can experiment as time goes on to see which is best for you, **focus your mind**, relax the muscles of your face. We are not forcing anything here, just attending. This is not a workout, but a work within.

This means letting the body be, and attending to your inner world. No one else may enter. This is your private, unique territory, the space where prayer unfolds.

You will soon be aware of your breathing. And you may like to follow this for a few moments, checking that it is regular, not too deep, yet natural. Then allow it to continue on its own.

We are not composing ourselves in order to snooze or switch off! Far from it. We want to win an alert listening to this inner world, where the action, or inaction, is. At this moment, we are setting the stage. Dimming the lighting . . . .

"prayer is **entering into the depths of the heart**
and dwelling there in peace. . . ."

If we exercise ourselves in this Prayer of Silence for half an hour every other day to begin with—Monday, Wednesday, Friday—we will, bit by bit, discover from within what no one can teach from without:

"We do not *know* how to pray:
but there is a Spirit within who does. . . ."

September

September

a mystery of silence

Firstly, prayer is never our initiative: once we take over, then we cease to pray. For prayer is never busy, never *our* business.

We belong to the family of God, that is human kind. And prayer is our response as we begin to explore this relationship, within the Other and among ourselves. When first we come to life, we grow in awareness of the human family. Beginning with our own nuclear family, we slowly edge out, relating to the bigger world at large. This human family—to which we now belong—is necessarily engaged in encountering its Maker. And this encounter with our Mysterious Maker is the very stuff of life.

> Meister Eckhart says: "As God makes man,
> he gives to each His very Essence."

So that true prayer arises naturally within every human experience and in every human heart—responding to the mystery of receiving Life, attending to our unique role in its drama.

"Be silent, be still: know me as your Maker": this we call prayer.

In the first reading, a Carthusian monk is speaking to his novices about their prayer. They have come to the solitude of the charterhouse or monastery to seek the Silence of their Maker. Like us they are beginners: so much to learn. We have no monastery walls and little silence. But do not lose heart: there is a teacher within, no other than our very Maker himself. All we need do is to be *found* by our inner Silence. For this silent Maker is within each human heart awaiting our response, a simple yes to our existence. The story starts there, then step-by-step unfolds.

This takes practice; it will also mean patience and perseverance. Slowly, as we continue with our half hour silence, each day it will become more and more a familiar friend. Our mind churns less as the silence becomes more real.

For deep within our heart and mind lies that frontier where our Maker holds us in being, gives us life every second of the day, seeks us and cares for us, holds and cherishes us—all this he does by the Gift of Himself.

> Once we have heard this silence
> we thirst to find it again

a mystery of silence

It is not a question of *making* prayer
or even making silence

Silence is not contrived

When one comes before the Lord
with a mind full of images
with strong emotions
and one's thoughts still in movement
one realizes the need for silence

Yet this is *not* to be silent
It is merely covering up the noise
or shutting it up within ourselves

There is no need to *create* silence
for it is already there
It is simply a matter of letting it rise up
from within us

Once we have heard this silence
we thirst to find it again

A CARTHUSIAN
The Wound of Love

3

making a start

As we begin this journey together, keep in mind all those who also pray. Those who are praying now, as we pray; those who prayed long ago and are now fully aware of what they did and why they persevered. Among those praying now, we will imagine most are far more accomplished than ourselves, who take these first few staggering steps.

And yet, hear our Carthusian once more. This monk is seasoned in his praying over many years and yet he tells us firmly:

> prayer of its very nature is always a beginning
> our best approach is that of a beginner

What encouragement. We seem to have turned up at the right school, certainly for me. No entrance exam, no previous experience required. I can simply start from the here and now.

But what is this he is saying:

> each time we pray
> we witness creation

> each time we enter into our soul
> in quiet presence
> we are created from within
> by a life-giving surge of Being

The purpose of our attending to this inner silence is to encounter our Maker—not in a once-and-for-all confrontation, or dreaded judgement: we meet our Mysterious Maker in our making, now and again now, in a continuing life-giving commerce of love, each time we come to pray. Then each moment of our day.

A recent study of spirituality in children, conducted by two sociologists from Nottingham University, revealed how the young are vividly aware of their own inner world. Each child takes his own experience very seriously—and in the main secretly—each give it his own unique signature, so that no one account is ever duplicated.

We too will have shared their fearless exploration of what it is to be human, body and spirit. We must begin again, renewing our childhood wonder at the marvels all around us and especially within.

So that each time we pray, it is a new start and a new prayer. That is what we mean by encounter with our Maker: it is to attend to our making. For we are all still in the making.

4

making a start

Prayer of its very nature is always a beginning
our best approach
is that of a beginner

Each time we pray
we witness creation
in the freshness of the first morning

Each time we enter into our soul
in quiet presence
we are created from within
by a life-giving surge of Being

As a child we receive and discover in wonder
This is why we never tire of prayer
why it is always new

you cannot repeat prayer
you can only receive each new moment
in its utter newness
each new prayer

We do not *know* how to pray
but there is a Spirit within
who does

+ CYRIL

Each prayer is a new start. Each prayer is unique—you may not repeat a prayer, only accept this moment, now. And my prayer is not your prayer: your prayer is yours alone. Utterly unique, a reflection of this Making relationship in Love, moment by moment.

You see. It is all very simple. And terrifying. A challenge to live, to explore, to risk.

Come to this well of inner Silence. It is yours. Only you may tread this path. Of course, you do not have to come this way. But think what you will otherwise miss. A chance at last to address that deep, deep thirst you have always known.

Nervous? I surely am. So take it slowly. Peer over the lip of the well. I see nothing, just blackness going down and down. Fear grips me. There is nothing there: or, worse still, real danger lurks. This unknown darkness could overwhelm me, or tell me all I least wish to know.

Calm down. Your mind races needlessly. Still your heart. Here, all shall be well. Your well. A well of healing. Belonging only to you but attended lovingly by your Maker, the Other whom you long to know—who already knows and loves you intimately.

As your eyes grow accustomed, even from where you now stand, safely on *terra firma,* uncommitted, can you not begin to see a strange reflection? A face of sorts, or at least a Presence, gazing up. Inviting, smiling, welcoming.

Can that be a reflection? It looks familiar and unfamiliar. Certainly, I would like to know more.

Then lower your bucket. Explore this strange inner world that belongs to you alone. It is only yours: only you may come this way—alone.

Take the first step. And listen. Drop a pebble into the mysterious cool water below. Listen for its echo. But be still and have patience. No hurry, have no fear, your Maker is at hand.

And when you are ready, when he offers, drink deep. It has been a long wait and you are thirsty.

> Ask only
> and I will give you
> Living Water

well of Silence

Come to this well
of inner Silence
you alone may drink here
but first
peer down
into its cool depths

see a mysterious reflection
not your own
but the Source of All
looks up

lower your bucket
gently descending
into the cool waters

when you are ready
draw it up once more
and drink

Ask
and I will give you
Living Water

JOHN SKINNER
(based on John 4:10)

making Himself known by silence

How many wasted words in our modern world. It almost seems that we have finally lost all reverence for the amazing gift of language, which enables us to relate to each other both in each other's presence and at a distance. Words belong to our Silence: it is damaged by their misuse and neglect. How often do we join in the meaningless noise that surrounds us: is it to choke down our inner peace and silence? Are we that afraid to be silent and learn about true living?

Ignatius fastens upon Christ's silence which, he tells us, pleased the Father. A novel idea, for we think first of his teaching, his preaching, his parables. But for the major part of his life, all we know of the Son of Man is his silence. Yet this solitude in obscurity pleased his Father. For during these long years, he listened and communed in silence with his own inner world praying, planning, giving thanks for all that was his—all that he would give back to us; equally, he went out to others, learning, listening, encountering with wonder the myriad complexity of his teeming world.

John calls Jesus Word, Word uttered by the Father. Spoken to us, for us to hear, to comprehend our meaning from his. Keep my word, he tells his friends at the end of his life, and my Father and I will come and make our home with you (John 14:23). A promise to us all. But we must keep his word in our hearts in the silence.

Long ago, the hermits of the desert would take a psalm, a passage from Scripture and slowly revolve it in their minds conscious of God's presence—*lectio Divina,* so-called "Divine reading." We may do the same, for "he is present in us," as Ignatius tells us.

Allow each word its space, each phrase its echo in your mind and heart and memory—listen for its echo, its resonance. Play with meaning, allow it to ebb and flow. There are no rules here. All is experiment and free fall. New meanings emerge, and new depths discovered. One day this phrase will sing which yesterday was still; now this sudden rush of understanding, while another passage still seems dormant.

making Himself known by silence

Better be silent
and be
than speak without being

It is good to teach
if the teacher acts on his own teaching

There is in truth but a single master
one who spoke
and at the same time was

What he accomplished
in silence
was worthy of his Father

He who truly possesses the word of Jesus
can hear even his very silence

then he will be perfect
acting by his Word
who makes Himself known by His silence

Nothing is hidden from the Lord
even our secrets are close to him

So as we go about our work
let us always remember
that he dwells in us

And so we will be his temples
and he will be our God
present in us

For he *is* present in us
that is the plain truth of the matter
and it is precisely as we love him
that he will show himself
to our own eyes

IGNATIUS OF ANTIOCH
Letter to the Ephesians

October

October

prayer and Love

Shortly before we launched *Hear our Silence,* I asked the Prior of the English Carthusians if he would offer us our own invitation to the prayer of silence, open and inclusive to all. "Your Father lets the sun shine on all. . . ." His response we now refer to as our charter—just over 150 words of amazing vision and hope.

We must all pray. For praying is like breathing, natural and necessary: simply our total response to the mysterious gift of Life. We grow in wonder at the backdrop of life and energy that teems around us. And we know not only are we part of this living drama, but we alone can imbue it with sense and purpose. For in our communion with all living things, we ultimately reflect their total meaning as we continue to attend to the core mystery whence we begin and end—that is our relating self. Being known and becoming known by God: expressing this loving potential in all our daily relating, loving, living. It is our very becoming, the continual process of our birthing.

We do this first in the mysterious presence of our Maker, whom we need not name, merely grow to know in love. For if we continue to attend to our Maker, we will learn the simple truth that he is still Making us. We are by no means the finished article: there are repairs to be suffered, and much more is promised as our inner potential for growth and wholeness is slowly revealed. And our Maker is with us constantly in our making. Our re-making or "again-making," as Julian of Norwich has it:

> See I am in all things.
> See I do all things.
> See I never lift my hands off my own works, nor ever shall,
>   without end.

The train leaving from track one will always wait for us before it departs: the escalator is ready now for our foot to take that first step, trusting we will be carried forward upon our intended journey.

And it is in prayer that we most closely attend to this Life-giving encounter.

Prayer ✛ Love

Asking people to pray
is like telling the wind to blow
the ear to listen
the eye to see
We cannot not pray
anymore than not be
once given the gift of existence
We can only shut it out or deny it

Prayer is simply the conscious dimension of being
when it opens out to receive all that it is
gift
marvellously
gratuitously there
word of communion with all things
who hears their silence of wonder
adoration before Him who is
the source and end of all

Prayer is also the birthing of the person
the creative revelation each is called to become
the etching of a mysterious face
reflected by the Mystery we contemplate
the knowing of God
as we come to know ourselves
Spirit breathed
by the Thou who calls and loves

Silence then is the plenitude of the Word

Prayer ultimately is love

+ CYRIL
St. Hugh's Charterhouse
February 20, 1999

13

We have already seen how prayer is essentially God's business, not ours. He always initiates this unique relationship. We simply attend. But how are we to go about listening to his Silence?

Once again, we can be guided by our Carthusian master. And this text cries out for *lectio Divina* to plumb the depths of its meaning.

Begin with this simple statement about prayer: Prayer is entering into the depths of the heart and dwelling there in peace.

But that might be misleading, suggesting that prayer is purely passive, a snooze beside the pool on a lazy afternoon. In fact, prayer actively engages us at our deepest center, the ground of our being. For prayer is attending to our root relationship, the mysterious frontier that lies between our Maker and ourself.

Yet you must journey alone. I will merely stand in your way. This is your journey: it belongs to you alone. Its meaning yours. Open your heart to "the breathing of your deepest being."

Sometimes key words may stand upon the page, signaling their numinous message. But there is no hurry. Let the words speak, if they will. Yet they will not always be the same words, and their meaning will vary in shade and tone. One day a passage will sound comfort, another moment words of warning.

My reading becomes so much more than scanning print upon paper, this *lectio Divina* soaks into my soul as the dialogue takes on a vivid, living intercourse.

"The truth shall set you free."

In today's world, our reverence for the Word is under such extreme pressure. Words themselves are spun, they are poured into our ears until we grow deaf to meaning. We talk endlessly with little inner attention to what we wish to offer our neighbor. We smile at the latest text joke on our mobile and wonder who sent it and why. Words in this world belong to everyone and to nobody. We risk falling into the chaos of Babel.

Yet it is a chaos that may be stilled: if once we lay claim to the inner silence of our deepest heart.

attending to God

Attentiveness to the deepest Self
leads one beyond self
Attentiveness to self
attentiveness to God
are like two interdependent
complementary movements—
the breathing of our deepest being

Prayer is entering into the depths of the heart
and dwelling there in peace
listening that is receptive
responding to this mystery of faith

Attentiveness to God
is the work
of faith and love
its fruit is the union
of love and knowledge
to which it gives birth

God is not an object
towards which we look
God may only be known
by his own light
Attentiveness to God
is to be receptive to this divine light
rather than an activity of the intellect

It is above all poverty, faith
receptive emptiness, nakedness and freedom
It is the eyes that are open in the dark
the desire of love

If God illumines the attentive heart
with his light of peace
the shadows are not thereby dispelled
but these shadows become luminous
absence reveals itself as Transcendent Presence

A CARTHUSIAN
The Way of Silent Love

15

beyond self

Some people view self or the ego with deep suspicion. They feel that the spiritual journey should begin by abdicating self and eradicating the ego. They are wrong.

Humanity has two unique and splendidly defining characteristics: we laugh and we reflect. No other living creature has a sense of humor, can smile, laugh, and make jokes. No other animal reflects upon its predicament, is able to turn back upon itself and wonder. These two aspects of our human makeup set us apart from the whole spectrum of living creatures; they also hold the promise of change and of our salvation.

Now if I deny my ego, seek to crush it, deny its existence, then I am in denial of my entire human makeup. The ego is the centre of our self, and true enough I can become egocentric so that life begins and stops with me. But my ego is softened and altered as it relates to others: that is the whole point of the family, the extended family of groups, at work and play. I may not escape my ego, but I must avoid egotism.

And as I relate, in prayer, work and play, with the Other, my Maker, then the first duty I have is to give thanks for this gift of myself, this I that I am. To turn one's back on this unique gift, the loving donation of my Maker would be a crime indeed. The opposite must be true, that my life's task is to work with my self, rule my ego so that it serves its purpose, becoming wholly me.

My belief is that prayer serves the primary purpose of giving me back my own true self. By that I do not say a return to some whole self that I once had and have somehow lost or spoiled. An Eden metaphor. No, the way is ahead, "fare forward voyager": we are in the making, in safe hands, set to discover fully who we really are and who we might become. Some journey.

Our inner self is the most precious gift we have and hold. We alone may touch it, be touched there, own it uniquely as *mine.*

beyond self

In the silence of self
I encounter an Other
far greater than the I of me

As the seed pushes roots into soil
as its leaves reach out to sunlight
the self cannot help but expand
into the ground of the Other
discovering new life
opening ourselves to living love

JOHN SKINNER
November 1999

the seed of your planting

George Appleton, who died in 1990, was a pastor in London, a canon of St. Paul's Cathedral, a missionary in Burma for 20 years, Archbishop of Perth, and finally Archbishop of Jerusalem. Amid so much external, active work across the world, he remained a man of prayer and guided many along the same path. He wrote numerous books of prayers and meditation which are still held in great esteem. On the page opposite is an example of his simple, yet profound, approach to prayer. To me it sounds like a wonderful invitation.

Again we have affirmation of a solitary journey, a quest and search for self that will take all our courage and determination. It is a lone pilgrimage— lasting a lifetime—but not lonely. I alone can find my true self, no one else can perform this task. It is a dangerous labour, but its reward is infinite. I will discover much that I do not welcome about myself, my dark side, my wounded side, my resistance, my capacity for malice and falling away.

But if I persevere, I will come again and again to the spring of Life. Once more we touch on our fresh birthing. Here, in these Waters, we will be named again, or be told our true name, embrace our real self. And this truth will set me free, with the freedom to explore my full potential in order to embrace its expanding mystery—"that self, the *seed* of which you planted in me at my making."

Such is our quest in the prayer of silence, to face the reality of the me I truly am from my beginning, scarcely daring to guess who in the fullness of my days I may become.

the seed of your planting

Give me the candle
of your Spirit

as I go down
into the deeps
of my being

Show me the hidden things
the creatures of my dreams
the storehouse of forgotten memories
and hurts

Take me down
to the spring of Life
and tell me
my nature
and my name

Give me freedom to grow
so that I may become
that Self
the seed of which
you planted in me
at my making

Out of these deeps
I cry to you
my Maker
my Lord

GEORGE APPLETON

November

November

late have I loved you

Augustine lamented that he had begun his journey so late. This is the young African bishop writing the world's very first autobiography, his *Confessions*. Before his time, no one had had the courage to write down their own personal story. Man never considered himself an individual, merely an insignificant part of the whole jigsaw. And yet Christ's entire message is directed towards the individual: time and again he encounters a solitary person in need. It took 500 years for this message to be heard, for the mold of mankind's solidarity to be broken down so that the individual voice might be heard for the first time, his response recorded.

Augustine tells his inner story with fierce disregard for his own sensibilities. His self-examination is a ruthless quest, his judgments unsparing. When at last he turns to God in his late thirties, he cannot believe how foolish he has been. How could I have stood apart all this time?

We may all recognize this feeling and share the same misgiving. Speaking personally, I recognize only too well how I am constantly repeating his complaint. While Augustine appears to have found his God once and for all—and the encounter changes him, decisively—this was never so with me. I first read this passage when I was 17; 50 years later I am still a long way from the goal—or am I? This is the age-old quest, the never-ending pilgrimage toward home. Our journey never ends until we arrive. For the present, this *now,* we must simply persevere—in hope and trust, drawn on by love.

Yet if God is good, our total bliss, why do we not fall into his arms and rest there? Instead, we struggle to be free. We prefer to go our own way. Augustine confesses that he was continually pulled down by the world's charms, a false beauty which never satisfied his deepest heart. Yet within these very snares lies God's beauty veiled. Even so, they are insufficient to quench his inner thirst. The true lover of God seeks him first and him alone. All else pales.

"Your finger touches me: I surrender to your loving peace."

late have I loved you

So late have I loved you
Beauty—ancient yet so new
I have come to love you now
yet so late in the day

You were within me
but I was in the world outside myself

I sought you outside myself
wantonly misguided
I wallowed in the beauty of those creatures you had made

You were still with me
but I was not with you

The very beauty of the world kept me far from you
yet unless each one of them had all not been in you
they could have had no being

You called out to me
you cried my name
and at last you burst through my deafness

You flashed forth upon me
your light surrounded me
I was blind no more

You breathed your sweetness
and I drew breath

now I gasp for more
I tasted
now I hunger and thirst for you

Your finger touches me
I surrender to your loving peace

Saint Augustine
The Confessions

23

I have purposefully taken liberties with this reading: the opening cascade of John's Gospel in which he announces Christ, the Word, who speaks to us as individuals, one to one. This all too familiar passage is full of mystery. Yet, with repeated reading, we are in danger of letting it pass us by, it's fullest impact seriously diluted. Coming to it fresh today, we may perhaps at last glimpse more of what it has to tell us.

Words. We are so accustomed to words. They fill our day, delight our ear, cause our tongues endless pleasure. As the Irish have it, "there's nothing like a good craic." And true enough, words are one of God's greatest gifts to us. We need words to meet each other, greet and understand. Console, explain, bargain, mediate—command, plead and—alas—endlessly offend. But human words are friable, they fail us at every turn. We need to reverence them like fresh baked bread, still warm from the oven. How different it is with God.

He speaks his Word. One single Word. Then Silence.

Word is Flesh: all is said.

In his Son, whom he brings forth, in his Word which he utters, God says All.

Creation is uttered by the Word: "through him all things came into being."

Man is summed up in the Word: "the Word is made Flesh." God's whole creative outpouring is expressed in this One Word, his Son. The man we know as Jesus.

Jeshua, as Mary would have named him, was an unremarkable Jewish baby. A boy, born unnoticed during the reign of Herod.

The mystery of this Word, the complete utterance of God, was cloaked in silence. Disguised as a baby? Not at all: the baby is the silent Word. He is the message. The Son of God is Man. And later on, Jesus will conflate the two, always referring to himself as Son of Man.

Dwell in this. Son of Man. God's own expression of himself, his Son— by whom he knows and understands all that he is—is now Man. God has taken center stage in our human world.

before the first axle

Before the first axle turned was the Word
and the Word was with God
and the Word was God

He was with God at the start
for through him all things came into being
nothing is except by him

All that comes into being
has life in him
that life is the light of men
a light shining in darkness
a light that darkness can never quench

The Word is the true light
that lights in all men
he is coming into the world
he is in the world
the world that was made through him
and the world does not know him

He comes home to his own people
and they give him no welcome
but to all who recognize and smile at him
he gives them power to become children of God

The Word is made our Flesh
and dwells in us

based on JOHN 1:1–14

Contemplating, again in his silent presence, this mystery: God shares himself intimately with us; in absolute and unconditional Love, he dwells with us.

Without ceasing—for he is our Source, our Light, our Life.

Each word has a meaning. Banded together, words become load bearers, like a bridge spanning a river; people can trust their weight to it, confident that they can continue their journey in safety.

All being well, that is the theory. Yet our everyday experience of words is that they seem untrustworthy. We may look a word up in the dictionary where we find that words tend to carry many changing meanings. The more weight we would have them bear, the less likely they seem to hold true. Our bridges sometimes seem as balsa wood.

But this Word is unique. It bears all meaning. "I am the way—truth and Life."

That is because this Word is uttered uniquely by the Father and Source of all. And so this Word, the only Son of his Father and our Father, speaks all that we can possibly wish to hear and learn about God. "Philip, have you been with me all this while, and you haven't realized—when you see and talk to me, you see and know the Father, my Father and your Father" (John 14:8).

The Word has been spoken to each one of us, "This Word is the only true Light—he lights all of us." And so Irenæus assures us, "he is always present to mankind." He is present to me now as I sit and write these words. As you read this sentence from this same page, he is present to you.

What can I mean, what does Irenaeaeus want us to grasp? The nature of this presence is rooted in our very humanity. The Father generates his Son and loving him and being loved by him, he knows and loves himself—in every detail. As we are made, again by the Father, the same process seems to repeat: we are made by means of the Word, the Son of God utters us and we come to be. So now we are marked with his distinctive fingerprints—both human and divine.

"Now God has impregnated us with his own Divine Seed."

Word of God
Seed of Christ
sown in man

The Word of God
the only Son of the Father
is always present to mankind

He may never leave his work
that he has fashioned

He shapes it continually
in the loving knowledge
of his Father

For now he has impregnated us
with his own Divine Seed

IRENÆUS
(based on John 1:3–9)

27

Stay with this seed, the simple metaphor. We know once seed is sown, we need to water it. This seed then that Christ has sown in our hearts, how may we tend it? By attending to the mystery in silent prayer—then we will irrigate and nurture our deepest ground.

The Desert Fathers escaped the bustle and business of urban noise and went into the desert. Or rather, they went into deserted parts of Egypt where they found plenty of water. Antony, the first hermit and a towering model for all solitary people of prayer, eventually became a keen gardener. But not before he had cultivated all that was going on within.

One of the earliest prayers of these hermits and the prayer that came to dominate all others with its simplicity was the Jesus prayer.

Jesus
Son of Mary
Son of Man
mercy
on me

This mantra would be repeated at prayer and at work—even in their dreams—so that Christ's presence informed their every breath. "Now he has impregnated us with his own Divine Seed."

Once, at a workshop at Pleshey in Essex where the retreat movement was watered and nurtured by Evelyn Underhill, we were told about the Jesus prayer by a Londoner who had been a Carthusian monk at Parkminster. He said how at home he now was with the Jesus prayer, how it had sustained him in the desert and solitude of the monastery. Eventually, it "became part of me—so that I don't pray this prayer, it prays me."

I used the word *mantra*. This is often mistaken for something mechanical, a tire iron or can-opener. God needs no such devices: there are no techniques in true love. A mantra is like an icon—love at first sight. Remember, always *his* initiative. So that our mantra—and it may be as simple as his only name Jesus, *Jeshua,* is like a warmer at the bottom of the bed, a smile across the room, the clasp of a hand, the kiss lip to lip. And, again, none of our doing.

We listen to his Word, lovingly spoken, in the ground of the soul, in our prayer of silence.

Jesus prays in us

Jesus
Son of David
have mercy on me

This prayer may never be prayed
never answered
unless Jesus
Son of Man
had been born of his Mother
Mary
the Virgin

So that now it may be prayed
now and constantly
in our hearts

As the Word
Son of Man
is broken
Lovingly spoken
by his Spirit
in the ground of our soul

The Word is made Flesh
and dwells among us
Now

Jesus
Son of David
have mercy on me

MEISTER ECKHART
CYPRIAN SMITH
STEPHEN MANTZALOS

December

December

in our making
He oned us to Himself

We always expect to see things from our own perspective. That is quite natural, this is how we work. But every now and again, we may glimpse the picture from another angle, God's own vantage point.

Julian of Norwich, an English mystic, is full of such Divine insights. In her *Revelation of Divine Love* (ch. 58), God's game plan in becoming man is turned upside down:

> humanity's fair nature was first prepared for his own Son

Not a question of God becoming man, then walking in step alongside us. "As surely as he is endless and without beginning, so surely was it his endless purpose to make humankind." Why? For himself. And why ever would he wish to do so? So that he could make us companions, his friends, sharing the full riches of all that it is to be human and then leading us in such friendship to know and love his Father. In making mankind, says Julian, the Father pours out his Son, knowing himself now in the human family: we are to become sons and daughters of the Father in our brother, Christ. Now we may respond to God's love in kind: the Spirit of Love moves in us.

> By the power of this same precious bond we love our Maker—like him,
> praise him and thank him with joy that has no end

In the simplest of words, Julian offers us deep insight into the mystery of the silent baby born in poverty in Bethlehem. We find it strange, but each detail of this story is deliberate and well-chosen and according to plan. God gives himself universally—"he lights everyone who comes to this world." The invitation is offered to all. It cannot be special, for it is so ordinary, so commonplace. You could almost miss it and pass it by.

And we risk doing so, every day. So attend to this mystery of God made Man that we may become members of his family in the silence of his birth.

> In our making, he knitted us and oned us to himself
> Only in my prayer of silence may I make this truth mine.

in our making
He oned us to Himself

God
the blissful Trinity
is
everlasting being

as surely as he is endless
and without beginning
so surely was it his endless purpose
to make humankind

Yet humanity's fair nature
was first prepared
for his own Son
the second Person

Then when the chosen time came
by full accord of all the Trinity
he made us

all at once

and in our making
he knitted us
and oned us
to himself

And in this bond
we are kept
as clean and noble
as at the time of our making

And by the power of this same precious bond
we love our Maker
and like him
praise him
and thank him
with a joy
that has no end

JULIAN OF NORWICH
Revelation of Divine Love, ch. 58

Gift of God

One afternoon at Parkminster, I was working in the cloister orchard when the Prior came to find me and ask how I was faring. I told him how fascinated I was by their silent prayer, how I wished I could offer this same silence abroad.

I said that I thought many people outside were hungry, without beginning to understand the nature of their loss. Many others sought some way to deepen their prayer, make more sense of an inner world of spirit; yet again there seemed so little guidance or help. I begged him to talk with me about a book of prayer, its central meaning for our daily human round. Why not e-mail each other alternately to build some kind of framework for a book which I could then craft for publication. I was delighted when he agreed to my suggestion.

For six, maybe seven months, we persevered in a desultory manner, attempting to build a coherrent narrative around this precious, yet illusive, topic. Yet from the outset our communication seemed fatally flawed, as if his Carthusian silence should not be ruptured in this way. Finally, we agreed to end our faltering discourse.

Even so, some crumbs fell from the rich monk's table. One I have headed, *Gift of God,* landed as an offering just before Christmas.

Seventy plus spare words from our Carthusian master state in simple terms the gift that is ours is the meaning of Christmas. Prayer is reduced in all its poverty to a receptive attention to the gift of God himself. "In our making he oned us to himself": the breathtaking truth of relationship with our Father is that he shares his Son with us, refashioning us, respecting our unique individual signature as a person and so enabling us to fulfill all our promised potential. This is our life-task and it is fed by our praying.

God is Love, John tells us—meaning that as God deals with us he may only treat us as a Lover. And this Lover, supremely, gives himself to us.

All we may do is stand by our open door and welcome him in: the Gift, ours for the receiving. This is the kernel of our Living: "love is his meaning."

Gift of God

Put all pretence aside

feel free to receive
in all simplicity
the gift of God

Instead of believing that it is I who seek
I can be the one who is sought

This is what
Christmas
and the Incarnation
are all about

God coming
to seek us out in our very humanity
entering through the door of our everyday being
bringing a Word of love
mercy and hope

May the door be open
the gift welcomed

+ CYRIL
December 14, 1999

the Word is made our Flesh

Here is Augustine, the great Bishop of Hippo in North Africa, preaching to his Nubian congregation on Christmas Day a mere 500 years after Jesus' birth. In his early years, Augustine was a rhetor, a skilled orator paid by the Roman authority to foster Latin as the imperial language. Today, English as a foreign language is taught across the world due to demand in the marketplace. In the Roman Empire, things were somewhat different. Latin was imposed across the territories as a sure means of binding it together. And rhetors were in place, like telephone engineers, to service the lines of communication. His words may seem both fulsome and compacted to our modern ear (he speaks in Latin). Yet, it seems to me, the more vantage points we have to view this Mystery of the God–Man, the better our chance to savor its awesome meaning. It is more than mere belief, more than a recognition that the Word is Flesh. For we as individuals are asked to do just as Mary did: hear the Word and cradle him in our womb. We too must *housel* him—the old English word for receiving Communion. We are invited on this day—and each moment of all our days— to receive him under our roof, to offer him our own hospitality. In exchange for this intimacy, not only are we offered back our humanity, unsullied, and sustained by his Love, day by day we are also called to explore and experience the rich potential of our unique human self. We are invited to wholeness. And such an invitation which Christ offers us by means of his Humanity points to, or rather compounds, our communion with the Divinity.

He restores the human race across all time. He uplifts his new family, offering us as one to his Father.

The Word is made our Flesh

The Lord through whom all things have been made
and who himself has been made center of all
he reveals his Father
yet creates his mother
Son of God by his Father without mother
Son of Man from his mother without father
Great day to Angels dusk to men
Word of God outside time
Word made flesh at his chosen time
He makes the sun only to be made under the sun
Disposing all time before his Father
he marks this moment in his mother's womb
In Him he resides as from her he goes forth
Maker of heaven and earth
he is born on earth under heaven
Wisdom too deep to tell see only this baby who sleeps
fulfilling the whole world he lies quiet in his crib
ruler of stars suckles his mother's breast
The Word is made our Flesh—today each day

SAINT AUGUSTINE
Sermon for Christmas

His Day Star leapt down

A mournful Christmas carol, *In the Deep Midwinter,* is voted England's favorite. I may be swimming against the tide, but for my liking its dirge-dreary tune and sentimental, sugary lyric sings all that is *not* Christmas.

Imagine for a moment some of Mary's feelings as she suckles her new-born son. Wonder and puzzlement must have been uppermost. "How has this happened to me? What does it all mean?" But then comes a flood of gratitude and overwhelming love at God's amazing, dynamic generosity to mankind— all centered in this tiny baby boy. She might scarcely have guessed how the whole world had been begun again by the baby boy she holds in her young mother's arms, this tiny infant whom she suckles at her breast. But looking back across the years, we can begin to perceive this enormous hinge of history.

Christ now stands at the center of our human family. So much for the plain fact: what is our response. For unless we collaborate and revise our life to accord with this Truth—God among us—we stand outside his stable, a mere onlooker to the greatest act of all time.

Winter's darkness is dispersed. The Father's Day Star brings us Light. Christ is now at the head of his table as we are all invited to join his feast, the feast of Life and Love. "In him we live and move, from him take we now our being." He is come to restore the human race across all time. He uplifts his new family, offering us as one with him to his Father. The Word is made our Flesh—today, each day. Let us join him at his feast.

His Day Star leapt down

At the silent turning of the night watch

his great Day Star
leapt down
from heaven to earth

the Word
was heard
by Mary

and she cradled him
in her womb

He comes now
to dispell our darkness
to fill us with new life

He calls us today
to live in peace
with ourselves
and with each other

We are now
children of God

The Word is made our Flesh
today

JOHN SKINNER
Christmas Day 2000

January

January

now

The new year always brings the worst out in me. I turn out of Christmas, get my breath back, and then begin to feel omnipotent. Well this year, I really will change, make lists that last, achieve a simple life-mending resolution that will transform me, make sense of all that has gone before.

Stop this cackle about future promises, change, resolutions of revolution. All we ever have is now. I repeat, say it again, so that I understand: all I am is now. What has passed is past. The past is only present in the present: the future is nothing until it arrives in the now. If I am continually fretting about time past and time future, I will never live my life which can only be in the now.

What better day to announce my now than January 1, 12:01 a.m. Time to wake up at last—to time. To the simple fact that it doesn't really exist, except to haunt me. *Now* is real because it is beyond time; like all real moments, they escape time and space.

The mystery of the gift of life is most admired by those who feel it is slipping through their fingers. The terminally sick (we all are), the prisoner deprived of his freedom (I too lack courage to be free), the poor (if once I might surrender some of the many tethers that rope me down). Whatever the human condition, we all share its basic ingredient: we are constrained to this precise moment. That is all we know, this now is all I can count on. Then use it. Savor the full measure of its meaning, its potency, its liveliness, its beauty, the gift it bears me.

So: January 1 brings me now. There is no guarantee that a full year is mine to follow; tomorrow and the day after all set out as white pages in my diary, ready to be inscribed. Count upon nothing apart from this moment in time, this precious gift of life, my life—***now.*** As my dear friend, Zez, who is in prison, always urges me: *carpe diem*. Take this day as yours and own it. There speaks wisdom: and I, who am almost fifty years his elder, hear it for the first time.

now

Prayer is the art of the now

We can only meet God now
it is now that he meets us

God doesn't come to us
in some future heaven—
He loves us now
wants us now
meets us now

This we call prayer—
believing in his love
receiving his love
resting in his presence
now . . .

this silent moment

JOHN SKINNER

nada

One of the great pathfinders of prayer is John of the Cross. This sixteenth-century Carmelite was a close friend and collaborator with the great Teresa of Avila. Together they set about reforming their Carmelite Order of both nuns and friars. And the cornerstone of their reform was prayer.

John speaks of the Dark Night of the Soul and of the nothing, or *nada,* that must be endured as we make our approach to God. In his ministry with nuns, he would sketch a kind of spiritual map on countless pieces of card. And it was always the same picture, a formidable mountain to be scaled, and from top to bottom, he would scrawl his motto—*nada, nada, nada*—a kind a repeating mantra of determination.

He was the third boy in an impoverished family. His father died when John was only a baby and his mother had a terrible struggle to keep her family together, clothed, and fed. As a young boy of nine, he was sent to a special school for poor boys at Medina del Campo; and by fifteen, he was a porter in the local hospital caring for the chronic sick and dying. Here he learned how suffering and love go hand in hand, an experience that led him to join the Carmelites where he met Teresa, a woman twice his age.

No sooner had John joined forces with Teresa and her reform movement, than his own brethren turned on him and locked him in a small airless cell for nine long months. He suffered this appalling incarceration with patience (he was allowed out in the open air for just 30 minutes each day that passed), yet this experience saw the gestation of his *Canticle,* the first of his great love poems echoing Solomon's *Song of Songs.*

The darkness of his prison cell, the physical and mental abuse from those who called themselves his brothers, his inner darkness and apparent exclusion by God: John endured them all and then burst free, a new man full of compassion for his fellows and brimming with the certainty of God's love for us all.

nada

So as to taste the best
learn the taste of nothing

So as to own all
let go of everything

So as to become who you are
walk away from yourself

So as to become wise
forget all you ever knew

So as to arrive at where you are not
you must walk the path of a nobody

JOHN OF THE CROSS

I will take away their heart of stone
and give them hearts of flesh

EZEKIEL 11:19

45

Another great teacher and guide in prayer is Meister Eckhart, the thirteenth-century German mystic and scholar. This gifted Dominican was revered as administrator, teacher, and preacher. His writings, though suspect in their day, are becoming increasingly recognized for their true worth. Here is "a voice, crying in the wilderness," a prophet for our times.

Eckhart's own day, like ours, was seeming apocalyptic, the civilization we have come to rely on slipping beyond our grasp, no longer in control. His response was not political but spiritual. Inhabit the great unknown within the human heart and spirit and truth will win the day.

The aspect that most appeals to me about Eckhart is his preaching. His sermons were electric. They soon became a must for the people of Cologne where he lived and taught for many years. They were written down, not by their author, but by people in his audience who realized what special words flowed, how precious was his message Sunday by Sunday.

In our reading, he propounds a method—some ancients might have named it a ladder—for prayer. Yet it is not a mechanical device aimed at lifting us to our Maker. Eckhart is more practical, more of a realist. He simply proposes a series of priorities for us to work at. A lifelong task.

First, we have to free ourselves from all the ties we have that surround us and immunize us from reality. Our "comfort zone," if you like, which modern people are so adept at constructing—fast food, instant entertainment, insurances against pain or even discomfort of every conceivable kind. We each must make our list. Then let go: sidestep them. Get on with real living.

Second, we have to receive. Make ourselves an open receptacle, yes—a womb. Remember Christ's words to Nicodemus which so puzzled him that he asked: "Must a man enter his mother's womb for a second time?" In a way, the answer is yes: we must lay ourselves open to being made again. Not a "makeover," in modern parlance, a quick fix to suit our own needs—but a radical rebuild designed by the One who only knows our true needs, our Maker.

Such is Eckhart's message: it beguiled and dazzled the people of Cologne; now it is our turn to respond.

as I pray

As I pray
I ask for freedom
from my greedy self
from the grip of all things

As I pray
I ask to be made again
by my Goodly Maker

As I pray
I seek that thirst
deep in my soul
that calls to him
my only true goal
As I pray
I fall silent
dazzled by total Love
as yet Unspoken

JOHN SKINNER
(after Eckhart)
July 2003

credo

The origin and purpose of our several creeds is to settle differences. The Nicene Creed buried the hatchet over centuries of squabbling about the reality of Christ. Today we use this peace formula liturgically. Sometimes even as a litmus test of our own orthodoxy. So it all gets a little muddied.

I want to suggest another approach. When I was working in the Downside library, quarrying monastic sources for my book *Wisdom of the Cloister,* I came across Saint Bruno's *Credo* and wondered what to make of it. Now, Bruno is the revered founder of the Carthusians whose desire to remain far from the public gaze led to the canonization of Hugh of Lincoln (who lived a century after him), well before that of their instigator. Bruno's creed goes in part:

> I believe firmly in the Father, the Son and the Holy Spirit:
> the Unbegotten Father,
> the only-begotten Son
> and the Holy Spirit who proceeds from them both.
> I believe these three persons are one God.

Such privately composed creeds began to occur around his time, the eleventh and twelfth centuries, and they served as a kind of last will and testament to their subject's faith and lifelong loyalty. Literally, they were uttered by or spoken over the dying person, consigning their faithful spirit into life eternal. An echo of Christ's own last words—"into your hands, Father, I breathe my Spirit."

So in one way they functioned like our familiar liturgical creed, as a solemn demonstration of right faith. But they went a step further; they uttered a final prayer which, like a will, disposed of this soul's last remaining possession, oneself, in order to hand it across the great frontier of death into new life.

I have set out my own version and encourage others to play with such an exercise. It bears more upon our praying than upon our dying. For in all our praying—which is always Trinitarian—we strive always to be present to ourself, who we really are, and who we reach out to in the silent encounter.

Who addresses us in our prayer? who is it who touches us to the quick? How may we respond, now?

"From him comes all paternity, in heaven and on earth."

credo

I believe
in my One and only Father
the Other
who gives me life

I believe his only Son
the Word
who speaks in my heart

he is Son of Man
mother
healer
elder brother

I believe he lights all mankind
sharing our burdens
healing our wounds
feeding our hope
fulfilling our potential
according to his game plan

I believe their Love
between Them
is poured out upon us all

we receive this Love
into our hearts
to share with all in need

May we believe this
as we live
together
Amen

JOHN SKINNER
December 2001

49

February

February

getting real

"Human kind cannot bear very much reality. . . ." Eliot's wonderfully reso-
nant throwaway line—from his *Four Quartets.* It sums up for me our stub-
born resistance to life, to love, to the Divine encounter. Why *do* we continually
fight shy of living our lives to the full? Why do we simply find it hard to experience the joy of being alive? Rowan Williams observes how we have turned
our backs on Christian joy and rush now to anything that can possibly distract us, detain us, perhaps for a few brief moments, before we pass onto
another empty bauble promising to cheat us away from being real.

But in silent prayer there is nowhere to hide, no fig leaf for our fear.
When we attend to our inner self that is all we have. And we may begin to
experience true poverty and all its accompanying riches. For if I am brave
enough to come to my senses, realize that I have nothing of my own, then I
am ready to receive all that is in waiting for me, all that truly belongs to me.

> "Your heavenly Father knows all your needs. First set your hearts on
> his kingdom, and all these will be given you as well. Do not worry
> about tomorrow: tomorrow will take care of itself."

If we learn to keep it simple, suddenly life comes back sharply into focus.
Life is supremely worth living, a stunning gift, here and now from our Maker,
full of purpose, brimming with potency and promise. And it belongs to me!

getting real

Human kind
cannot bear
very much reality

Getting real
can be such a painful experience
staying real
hurts

We fight shy
of the beauty
the reality
of life
shrink from welcoming
its vibrant challenge

In our Silence
we may find the courage we need
to accept
all that is on offer
as we say

I am
thank you
Father
for
my being
me

JOHN SKINNER
January 10, 2002

See a horse pace its field, then lift its head and gallop—all for the fun of it. Spot a cat leap onto the sofa and curl up in complete comfort. Picture essays in life, in animal life that is incapable of self-reflection. Only I can rejoice in the beauty of movement, the vitality of a living creature. The cat, the horse just do it!

How seldom do I own my life in all its beauty. The ability to feel, hear, smell, use this pair of hands with purpose and assured dexterity. The artist does it all the while: why don't I? When she was about seven, our daughter, Hatty, was trying much patience yet again. So I told her straight: "Hatty, pull yourself together, use your head! What do you think God gave you a head for?" "For my senses, of course, Dad." Her reply, swift and sure, knocked me off balance. Seven-year-old Hatty rejoiced already in the "fearful symmetry" of her head. Eyes, ears, nose, tongue and taste were all hers to use: and that felt good to her.

When we first come to Silent Prayer, the senses seem to stand in the way. Noises sound unusually loud and intrusive; my head seems buzzing with all kinds of distractions that take me everywhere rather than here, where I want to be. But after a little practice and perseverance, this will fade. My silence becomes a kind of chamber, a favorite retreat familiar to me.

As I learn to slow things down and welcome this descent inward, the body and the senses seem to capitulate, abandoning their protest. Of course, there will be wretched days, when the whole idea seems ridiculous. But stay with it. That will pass.

When my Silent Prayer stills me, it brings me back to myself. I come to sense within who I really am. This is the true gift of my prayer.

Giver of Life

Each breath
I take
every moment
received
brims
full of life
clear
and sparkling

Gifting me
this moment
now

Beaker
of transparent
limpid life

Clear for me
to colour
sparkling
with expectation

All my life
is in this moment
Now—
Gift of
the Giver of Life

Drink
to the full
and
thirst
no more

JOHN SKINNER
January 2002

So what have I learned about my praying so far?

First is that it is part of me. I have been at it long enough, and yet how far have I come? Wrong question: we never make much palpable progress, simply because prayer is not a road or track to pass along but a relationship—given to us continually and to which we respond from moment to moment, day to day. All I can say about my prayer is that if I leave it to one side, I suffer, I am no longer myself. I can stagger on for a while pretending nothing is awry, but then I find that I must return to my Silence, this hidden well of my being.

There I find the Silent Word. He, too, is weary by this well, weary of my deafness, my reluctance, my resistance. But this Word, always speaking in the eternal Silence, utters one Word—Love—and he speaks to me. Always. If only I listen, I will hear.

There is a wonderfully endearing passage in Julian of Norwich where she writes about her own experience of prayer:

> For many times our trust is not complete; we are not sure whether God hears us, or so it seems, due to our unworthiness and we feel quite empty. How often are we barren and dry at prayer, sometimes seeming even more so when they are done. Yet this is only in our feelings and caused by our own folly coming from weakness: I have felt as much myself.
>
> And among all this confusion of thoughts, our Lord suddenly came to mind and showed me these words, saying:
>
> "I am the ground of your beseeking: first it is my will that you have it, and then I make you want it: now since I make you seek, and then you do seek, how should it then be that you should not have whom you seek?"

I find it endearing simply because my great anchorite, who spent decades in her cell in Norwich at prayer, is still able to describe her own wrestling and confusion. But then she provides us with the perfect answer: "I am the ground of your beseeking. . . ."

What we seek, we never lost: our quarry is also our hunter—that is precisely what love is about.

hearing Silence

The Father

speaks
one Word
who is
his Son

This Word

he speaks
always
in
eternal silence

In that Silence

our soul
must listen—
will
hear

JOHN OF THE CROSS
Canticle

our Way of Life

I have described my experience of living with the Carthusians at Parkminster.

They were generous; inviting me to visit their monastery, even more giving when they invited me to stay and for two precious weeks live their life alongside them. For they are serious about their silence and speak of guarding their solitude: with these two basic bricks they build their monastic life.

I was sitting with the Prior one afternoon. (At his suggestion we would come together every third day to check that I was surviving.) As the second week turned, I knew time was running out; and this afternoon, I plucked up courage and asked: "Tell me about prayer."

"Prayer is a way of life," came the disappointing answer. I had hoped for more, after all, here was a man forty years seasoned in praying. Was this all he had to say? At the time, I felt empty-handed, short-changed. But then I began to realize that this is all we can say about prayer. It is so important, it should be my way of life!

So how can prayer become my way of life? How may I spread this Silence across my day, making it permeate all that I do? First, by remaining faithful to the Silence itself, taking it seriously, making it real each day. And from this well of silence I may draw energy and reality for all that follows, all my actions, my relationships, the decisions, disappointments, setbacks, and joys that flow through my day.

For deep within, I am aware of a still center, a source of inner energy that is given to me, the gift of Life that is Love. This I can touch, or rather be touched by any and every moment, and especially *now.*

If this becomes my way of life, I shall be fully alive as my Maker always intended. The table of life is always prepared, all I may do is sit and sup.

How have I been resistant so long?

our Way of Life

With every breath we draw
we know the mystery of the Father
who continually pours out
his gift of Life

Beside this well of life
we encounter the Word
his Son
who yields his own Promise
of Living Water
the Spirit of his Love

Drinking this Living Water
poured out for us in Love
is our task
and joy
in the Prayer of Silence

Our Way of Life

JOHN SKINNER
August 23, 2000

March

March

our Maker Keeper Lover

I have chosen Julian of Norwich, a great English mystic, to be our guide through the Easter Mysteries. On May 8, 1373, she tells us that she was overcome by a fever which quickly turned into a paralysis spreading through her body. Over the course of a week, she then experienced a succession of "showings" or visions, many of them pertaining to Christ's own sufferings and death.

Julian did not die. She recovered to become an anchorite and dwelt on her visions for the next twenty and more years. We do not know her name but now call her by the dedication of the little church in Norwich to which her hermitage was attached. Today it is her shrine.

In the very first showing, her own near-death sufferings are linked directly to her dying Lord. The priest has come to annoint her and a boy brings in the crucifix. She cannot take her eyes away from this image, so real is it to her. But in the midst of her pain, she is comforted by the suffering Christ, a replay of the Good Thief on Calvary. Love abounds: this is for real, she tells us. And then the startling switch— "suddenly the Trinity filled my whole heart full of utmost joy."

At first reading, this sudden juxtaposition seems uncomfortable, even inappropriate. Yet Julian's meaning soon becomes plain. The Trinity is working wherever God is: both here with this dying woman, and, most surely, as his Son hangs dying. In more detail, his love is ever present in each detail of our day-to-day lives, active, dynamic, purposeful.

Elsewhere we read:

> See I am God.
> See I am in all things.
> See I do all things.
> See I never lift my hands off my own works, nor ever shall, without end.
> See I lead all thing to the end I ordained for it from without beginning with the same might, wisdom and love that I made it.
> How should anything be amiss?

This early passage from Julian's *Revelation of Divine Love* with its bold and original leaps is a frequent characteristic of her writing; but most typical is her confidence in God's intimate and caring love for every one of his human family.

our Maker Keeper Lover

Now at once I saw red blood trickling down from under the
garland
Hot and freely it fell
copious and real it was
as if it had just been pressed down upon his blessed head
who is truly both God and man
the very same that suffered thus for me

Within this same showing
suddenly the Trinity filled my whole heart full of utmost joy
I knew then that heaven would be like this for all who come to it
without end

For the Trinity is God
and God is the Trinity
The Trinity is our maker and keeper
The Trinity is our everlasting lover
everlasting joy and bliss
by our Lord Jesus Christ

JULIAN OF NORWICH
Revelation of Divine Love, ch. 4

Julian's whole life experience, her near-death illness and her subsequent years of prayer and contemplation, she sums up in one phrase—"Love is his meaning." An echo of John's own summation, "God is Love": a meaning for us today.

Writing in Middle English, Julian is our very first woman author and a contemporary of Chaucer, whom she frequently rivals for vivid imagery. What could match her wonderful metaphor of God's ever present, "homely" Love for us all. "He is our clothing that lovingly wraps and folds us about. It embraces us and closes us all around. . . ." And note the "us." Julian continually makes it plain that her experiences, remarkable as they are—and they took her a lifetime to digest and hand on to us—are given for us all. "This was shown for all my even Christians," as she puts it.

So God's love is as comfortable as our clothing and for everyday wear—"it hangs upon us with such tender love." I have a Carthusian friend whose motto and daily war cry is "Keep it simple." Julian would approve. For how we love to complicate and walk away from the plain and obvious truth about God's relationship with us.

We gaze at the crucifix and think of sin. We look away in guilt, saying, "We did this to him." But this is not how Julian sees things. "I saw that he is the ground," our ground where we may safely plant our feet. Again her dazzling metaphor, boldly invites our trust. The sufferings of Christ are not merely part of our own experience of living, they are at the center. Why, because they give meaning to our muddle. And let's not call it sin: *muddle* is a better word to describe our blind and feeble attempts to make sense that we belong in this, his human family.

But once we place Christ, suffering for love of us all, in the center again, everything comes back into focus. "For truly, he can never leave us. This made me see that he is for us everything that is good."

He is the ground

While I still had sight
of our Lord's head as it bled
he showed me
further understanding
of his intimate and homely love

I saw
that he is the ground
of all that is good
and supporting for us

He is our clothing
that lovingly wraps
and folds us about
it embraces us
and closes us all around
as it hangs upon us
with such tender love

for truly he can never leave us

This made me see
that he is for us
everything
that is good

JULIAN OF NORWICH
Revelation of Divine Love, ch. 5

clothed in the goodness of God

I mentioned Chaucer and suggested that Julian is many times his equal with her poetic imagery. As she waited in her hermit's cell for her overwhelming visions to settle and become clear water fit to drink, Julian circles again and again her key ideas. The musical rhythm of her words reflect the eloquence of spoken English as it too was emerging and starting to flow in her day. "For his goodness fills all his creatures and spills into all that he does."

In this next reading, she returns to the idea of God's intimate and homely love being like our clothing. She develops what had been an external image—clothing hanging lovingly upon us, protecting, warming—to an inverted, interior expression.

As if clothing were not sufficiently homely, she offers us an X-ray image of God's love: "For just as the body is clad in clothes and the flesh in skin and the bones in flesh with the heart in the breast, so are we soul and body clothed and wrapped around in the goodness of God."

And the loving invitation to intimacy with our Maker, Keeper, Lover is further domesticated with yet more startling imagery. "He is our endless home. . . ." Think of your dream house, fashion all that you will—number of rooms, garden, and so on. All this is yours to dwell in "endlessly." Too good to be true? Not at all, this, Julian insists, is our reality. Now and for all time. "For the goodness of God is the highest prayer. . . ."

Not our own prayer, but Christ's prayer, "*The* highest": so that it is surely heard. "It comes down to us to meet our very least need."

Her punchline of the whole piece comes now: "It quickens our soul and brings it to life." This echoes her opening phrase and complements it: "For his goodness fills all his creatures and spills into all that he does."

Again, Julian experiences God's love as a continuing daily activity. He is with us in all that we do, guiding, directing, enabling. No wonder her images are so rich, clashing forth like ceaseless waves upon the seashore, sounding out her simple message.

Love is his meaning. Our homecoming.

clothed in the goodness of God

For his goodness fills all his creatures
and spills into all that he does

He is our endless home
he only made us for himself
he remakes us by his blessed passion
and always keeps us in his blessed love
All this is down to his goodness
For the goodness of God
is the highest prayer
and it comes down to us
to meet our very least need

It quickens our soul
and brings it to life

For just as the body is clad in clothes
and the flesh in skin
and the bones in flesh with the heart in the breast
so are we
soul and body
clothed and wrapped around
in the goodness of God

Yet the goodness of God
is always whole
and more near to us
without any comparison

Our dearest kindly will
is to have God
and his good will
is to have us

JULIAN OF NORWICH
Revelation of Divine Love, ch. 6

We now come to the passage that is so well known that it is often misinterpreted. The hazelnut. "He showed me something small, about the size of a hazelnut, that seemed to lie in my hand, as round as a tiny ball."

The stream-like flow of her words . . . let them not beguile. Let's stay with her meaning. "This is all that is made," something tiny, a hazelnut in the palm of my hand is the sum total of creation. Or rather, is not the palm, on which the nut rolls precariously, our Maker's outstretched hand? As he gazes at this little thing—so tiny compared to our Mysterious Maker—all he knows is his Love. "This is all that is made. This lasts. And it will go on lasting forever." Not to say our material world is immortal and unchanging. Not at all. The only unchanging ground is our Maker's love for us: "so it is with every being that God loves." We will last because God loves us and causes us to respond to his love by receiving all that he offers.

And Julian explains the Divine economy, his "working" which is his invitation to us. "I saw three properties about this tiny object. . . ." (Let yourself be this tiny object.) "God had made it. God loves it. God keeps it." She returns to the dynamic Trinity, lovingly involved in our human family. A mystery she may not, cannot spell out. "Yet what this really means to me—the Maker, the Keeper, the Lover—I cannot begin to tell."

The answer is: there *is* no answer—beyond receiving his Love in our prayer of Silence; remembering we are as a rolling hazelnut in his loving palm, balanced precariously yet preciously "until we are fully one with him."

only in you I have all

He showed me something small
about the size of a hazelnut
that seemed to lie in the palm of my hand
as round as a tiny ball

This is all that is made
This lasts and it will go on lasting forever
because God loves it
And so it is with every being
that God loves

I saw three properties about this tiny object
God had made it
God loves it
God keeps it

Yet what this really means to me
the Maker
the Keeper
the Lover
I cannot begin to tell
For until I am fully one with him
I can never have full rest nor true bliss

God of your goodness
give me yourself
for you are enough to me
and I may nothing ask that is less
that may be full worship to you
And if I ask anything that is less
I am ever left wanting
but only in you I have all

JULIAN OF NORWICH
Revelation of Divine Love, ch. 6

April

April

pain gain

I have a friend in prison who invites me in to talk week by week. Two hours at a time: we know each other pretty well by now. There is a great deal I have come to know and admire about Zez. The first is his ability to live in the present, now, without much bitterness as to his lot (he's just 24 and has nine months left to serve of a seven-year sentence). The second is his generosity toward his fellows. We were in the visiting hall last week when Zez looks across and greets a man. I asked about him and was told he was Kurdish, a refugee who had landed up in prison and had been released two months before. "I helped him out. . . ." Zez volunteered. I pressed him. "He was being bullied so I sorted them out. Got me into a spot of trouble, but it was worth it."

That's Zez all over. When he speaks of pain, he reminds me of a courageous fullback on the rugby field—a high kick is coming his way plus half the opposition threatening to arrive all at the same time. He stands his ground, eye on the ball. Pain always has a purpose, he tells me, it's a kind of gift that will teach us a special lesson if only we are willing to listen: "stay with the pain, ride it to see where it leads. It always pays off. . . ."

Of course, processing our pains is never instantaneous. We have a family saying, "on the third day." Take a child to the doctor with some incipient malady: "Give it 48 hours," he will advise, "and then let's see what we have. . . ." It will either pass over or the illness will manifest itself in a recognizable form—on the third day. It is the same with antibiotics or a course of any medicine: you start taking your pills and nothing seem to change . . . until the third day.

Likewise with our pains and trials; if we stay with them, there will come a third day.

pain gain

Let me stay with this pain
not turn away
but receive it as your gift

Trace back its roots
to long ago
find its thread of meaning

Water those roots
with tears if needs be
but never with pity of self

Befriend my pain
own my pain
come to dwell in our pain

Wait until the Third Day
for my pain
to turn
to Joy

JOHN SKINNER
(for Zezzy)
May 2003

the stream of Life

Thomas Traherne lived through the middle of the seventeenth century; son of a shoemaker in Hereford, he and his younger brother were early orphans. Reared by their wealthy uncle, both received a thorough education—Thomas graduating from Brasenose College, Oxford, in October 1656. He first served as rector at Credenhill in Herefordshire; but less than a decade later, he became chaplain to Sir Orlando Bridgeman, Keeper of the Great Seal, who had his households in London and upstream along the Thames in Teddington, Middlesex.

He wrote extensively—many poems and lengthy, pious meditations. At the time of his death, he was working on an ambitious encyclopedia which he intended would show "all things to be objects of happiness." In recent times, his work has gained more and more attention—Penguin Classics publishes a handsome helping of his writings and few of his poems were beautifully set to music by Gerald Finzi.

Mystic, seeker, and lyrical writer, his life bears some similarities to Julian of Norwich even down to the loss of his final work until its recovery some twenty years ago.

Here he speaks as Julian, from his own prayerful experience of the Trinity—mystery beyond spelling, yet spilling into our living. All prayer is Trinitarian, that is to say it begins and ends in love. For me, prayer is about reaching inward to my Maker, who makes me in love, keeps me in love, and wishes me to grow to my true self in love. Unless I know this, my most profound and original relationship, nothing else makes sense. But once glimpsed, all my other relationships come into focus.

And if I tap into the Fountain, or, allow the Stream to flow within, then I am given back to myself, the real me, not the ego I would like to act out. And once the fig leaf falls away, I am able to stand naked before my Maker and hold my ground without fear—for what is there to fear in Love? Love is his meaning: and we were made for it.

the stream of Life

In all love there is a love begetting
a love begotten
and a love proceeding
Love in the fountain
and love in the stream
are both the same
Therefore they are both equal
in time and glory

For love communicates itself
therefore love in the fountain
is the very same love
communicated to its object

Love in the fountain
is love in the stream
and love in the stream
equally glorious with love in the fountain

THOMAS TRAHERNE
Centuries of Meditations

Saint Bruno charged his Carthusians to be masters of silence, guardians of solitude.

Born in Cologne around 1028, his career began as a precocious scholar at Rheims, one of Europe's leading universities. At the end of his studies, Bruno was appointed assistant professor and soon afterward was elected Canon of the Cathedral Chapter. By 1056, barely thirteen years after entering the schools, he was both rector and their principal.

His tenure was noted for his brilliance both as teacher and administrator. But there came a bitter dispute with a new archbishop, the corrupt Manasseh, who deprived him of his office, his goods and forced him into exile. From that moment, Bruno turned aside from the world of ambition, fame, and high office to seek the reality behind them.

Characteristically, he has left us little of his writings: a couple of letters and a few brief sayings. Unlike most spiritual masters who wish to communicate their wisdom in writing, Bruno remains silent. But of course that is precisely what he did leave us—the potency of silence.

"The fruit that silence brings is known to him who has experienced it": his words have the ring of a Zen aphorism, stating a proposition, then unsaying it. But our contemporary Carthusian author spells it out well, so that we begin to hear the silence, hunger after its meaning. It is something like missing the church clock's chimes and then counting them on the echo.

We can easily dismiss silence as something negative, a hostile silence. But that is because we fear its very power. I remember being in a sauna once when in came two young girls. After a moment, one turned to her friend and complained, "It's awfully quiet in here." They were not used to being silent, being still, and it was unnerving to come upon it unexpectedly.

We cannot make silence or go to meet it halfway. Silence is within and with us always. For true silence, silence that "brings us fruit" is the silent presence of our Maker, the guiding finger of our Again-Maker, Christ, the loving whisper of their mutual Love for each one of us.

Receive in silence, again and again. And especially now.

listening to the Word within

Silence is a listening
not the feverish expectation of a word
that might fill our heart

but a calm receptivity
to him who is present
who works noiselessly
in our innermost being

Silence
combines the absence of words on the lips
and in the heart
with a living dialogue with the Lord

"The fruit that silence brings
is known to him
who has experienced it"

This is Silence
to let the Lord utter within us
a word equal to himself

Reaching us without our knowing how
the very Word of God
comes
and resonates
in our heart

A CARTHUSIAN
The Wound of Love
(quotation from St. Bruno)

He is the means of all our glory

To continue with Traherne's passage on the Trinity . . .

I always think the Creed with its reference to Christ "sitting at the right hand of God the Father" is so distancing. But then we are looking at a theological peace treaty, not a spiritual exposition. Traherne feels safe when dealing with the Trinity; he does so willingly and with an air of familiarity, thereby demonstrating how often he has dwelt upon the Mystery. Or possibly, if he were to answer for himself, he might turn that on its head and declare that the Trinity dwells with him—within him.

For this is the essential handle to grasp: God can never distance himself from his creatures. He made us in Love—which is the only manner in which he may deal. He dwells within us in Love—for love is self-giving and Absolute Love gives Himself within his creature.

And this self giving is achieved by means of his Son, his Word whom he speaks within our heart. "This Person did God, by loving us, beget—that he might be the means of all our glory."

Begetting is a wonderful word, ancient, yet still fresh. For it says exactly as it does: the Father gets us to be, to become, and to persist in being. And his loving gift of creation should not be seen as a once-and-for-all act, like a child winding up a mechanical toy and setting it down on the playroom linoleum. Our Father makes us and is still making us all the while, holding us lovingly in his arms. The Again-Maker, his Son, is also active; through the power of his living manhood we become more ourselves, adding our own unique contribution to our human family, yet all the while reflecting his glory. The stuff of our life . . . why we are here.

He is the means of all our glory

This Person is the Son of God
who
as he is
the Wisdom of the Father
so is he
the Love of the Father

For the Love of the Father
is
the Wisdom of the Father

And this Person
did God
by loving us
beget
that he might be
the means of all our glory

THOMAS TRAHERNE
Centuries of Meditations

May

pied beauty

Not always our dour, Jesuit poet, let Hopkins sing in spring. His *Pied Beauty* has a Celtic ring that echoes his wonderful nature diaries. He loved to wander the fells above Stonyhurst and note—describe as well as sketch—all that he saw. God's face in nature's breathtaking beauty.

He sees diversity wherever he looks. At the sky reflected in the flank of a cow!

The trout in a stream, their camouflaged backs safeguarding them as they stand feeding in the clear flow. So introverted his vision that Hopkins all of a sudden is able to break loose into a far wider vision—"all trades, their gear, tackle and trim." But all the while, he perceives the source of this beguiling beauty as their unchanging Maker.

Spring is the year's resurrection. Winter thaws and green once more appears, vivid beyond my fondest memory when last I saw hawthorn, fresh grass pushing up under the mother ewe's swelling sides. And I thank Hopkins for his sensitivity, his pain in living so close to the edge as to speak to me about the pain and the beauty, pied, dappled, and mysterious. Yet so beguiling.

Welcome this spring. But welcome also to every spring-like change that offers me new life throughout the seasons. The marvel of Hopkins is his ability to observe and wonder. He did so magnificently when observing nature—a windhover (kestrel) on the wing, the memory of felled poplar trees. But he also met people in the same way: the interaction of two brothers whom he taught; one is on the stage performing in the school play, the other is wracked with his vicarious nerves as he watches in the audience.

An object lesson for me to be more alert so as to reflect upon the mystery that lies always just beneath the surface of my everyday existence.

As Blake puts it: "Turn but a stone and start an angel's wing."

Pied Beauty

Glory be to God for dappled things—

For skies couple-colour as a brinded cow;

For rose-moles all in stipple upon trout that swim;

Fresh-firecoal chestnut-falls; finches' wings;

Landscape plotted and pieced—fold, fallow, and plough;

And áll trádes, their gear and tackle and trim.

All things counter, original, spare, strange;

Whatever is fickle, freckled (who knows how?)

With swift, slow; sweet, sour; adazzle, dim;

He fathers-forth whose beauty is past change:

Praise him.

GERARD MANLEY HOPKINS

Time is one of our greatest mysteries. Seemingly a Divine gift, yet man-made. Endlessly squandered, precious beyond our reckoning. Time can fly, it can grow heavy in our hands and hearts, then suddenly it may evaporate—as man-time turns to sacred time. Time is beyond my control, but I must not let it take hold of me.

Setting mechanical time aside (time for tea, time to catch the train), I want to glimpse the magic of time. I first knew sacred time when my wife was in labor bearing our first son. Time stopped still, or did it belong to us alone? Two young, unknowing parents, on the brink of something mighty, together in a single task—enabling this new person to arrive. Was it four hours, five, or six? No matter, time went out of the window as we learned how to engage in the *now*.

When we are touched by love, by beauty, by a crisis that takes over, by a pain that will not leave us so that we must carry its load—time stops ticking and we live from moment to moment in a flux of *now*. Not always possible, never for us to contrive, but from time to time I may be able to spot the wave and hope to ride it when it comes.

sing me at morn

Sing me at morn
but only with your laugh

Even as Spring
that laugheth into leaf

Even as Love
that laugheth after Life

For Time
is man-made
yet your most precious gift

Let me not take time
let me not abuse time
seek to escape our time
or be used up by time
and myself wasted

Let not our time pass me by
but may I stay
in our Silence
between the tick and tock

Knowing your stillness
in the Process of time
your most precious Gift

JOHN SKINNER
(after Wilfrid Owen)
May 2003

Swami Abhishiktananda: what a name to wrestle with! We'll begin with the Swami, title of an Indian holy man, our first clue. And the long one simply means in Hindu—"bliss of the one who is annointed." And the name was taken by Henri le Saux, a French Benedictine, who left his community in France to explore the Hindu mystical tradition and attempt to reconcile it with traditional Western monasticism.

His courageous initiative was followed up by Bede Griffiths who, as it were, revealed the hidden path of his predecessor. Both men refused to be confined by their known traditions. Rather like Hillary and Tien Sing facing the wrath of Everest, determined to battle to its summit, they turned their backs on the safe life to embrace a life of risk and danger. Risk of nothing happening: danger of ridicule and rejection by those they had left behind.

But "the Spirit blows where he will." Bold men hear his call. "Follow me: come and see where I live, . . ." an ancient and familiar invitation. Sometimes heard, sometimes going unanswered. But it is a call to us all. We will all have to leave everything one day. If we can leave a little behind each day, that will be something. An opening of the door to the call to freedom of spirit, a freedom we all yearn for.

An invitation to explore our real self, not the fabricated false ego I massage and pretend is mine. We don't have to change our name, or our address, merely listen to each simple task and we will be led one step at a time to discover the miracle who is our true self. The gift he longs to bring us.

the only real Self

The Spirit blows where he will
he calls from within and from without

May his chosen ones never fail
to attend to his call
In the desert or in the jungle or in the world
the danger is always to fix one's attention upon oneself

For the wise man
who has discovered his true Self
there is no longer forest or town
clothes or nakedness
doing
or not-doing

He has the freedom of the Spirit
and through him
the Spirit works as he will
in this world
using equally
his silence and his speech
his solitude
and his presence in society

Having passed beyond
his own self
his own life
his own being and doing
he finds bliss and peace
in the Self alone
the only real Self

SWAMI ABHISHIKTANANDA

God in a point

At times, Julian can be breathtaking. "God in a point": how can that be? We think of his immensity, his absolute span of all creation, his power, his infinity. How can one boil this down to a point?

A point is the center of the circle from which all else is defined. When we "get a point," we say "the penny has dropped." The penny, in God's case, is that, like it or not he is at the epicenter of our life. This we can ignore, but we may not deny. All circles have centers: our center is God. *Point final,* I rest my case, as the French might say.

Well, not quite. Julian leads us in more persuasive ways. "I saw that he is in all things." This she saw so clearly, "in a point," that abruptly she was reminded of sin, the world's chaotic mess. If God is in all things, doing all things, even the very least, what of our human mess. "And as I marvelled quietly, a soft dread came over me . . . so that I asked, what is sin."

She describes sin as "no-deed," invisible compared to the reality of the Point. The vision of God at the point of all, the supreme agent of all activity and reality, is very obvious *notionally,* once we think about it. But we simply have to admit that it doesn't seem that way to our eyes.

Fine, says Julian, that's just the way it looks. Hold onto the Point. Which is that "our Lord does all . . . therefore I needs must recognize that all that is done, it is well done."

She is telling us that God, being the still point of all, his loving activity reaches out into every aspect of our existence, great or small—the mid-point of all things. Attend to this in our Silence and one day, we too may see the point a little more clearly.

God in a point

I saw God in a point
and in this sight
I saw that he is in all things

And as I marvelled quietly
a soft dread came over me
so that I asked in my mind
What is sin

For I saw clearly
that God does all things
even the very least

I knew truly that nothing happens by chance or accident
but all is by the foreseeing wisdom of God

Even if it seems by chance or accident in our sight
that is due to blindness or shortsightedness on our part

For these things are in God's foreseeing wisdom
from without beginning
indeed he leads them all rightfully gloriously continually
to their best end

yet as they come about
they fall upon us suddenly to take us unawares
we see them as misshaps or accidents;
but it is not like that with God

Therefore I needs must recognize
that all that is done
it is well done
for our Lord does all
But at this time creatures' deeds were not shown
but only our Lord working in the creature

For he is in the mid-point of all things
and he does all things
yet I was sure he did not sin
And here I saw truly that sin is no-deed
for in all this sin was never shown

JULIAN OF NORWICH
Revelation of Divine Love, ch. 11

June

June

the White Tiger

This stunning poem is both poignant and mysterious: written by the Welsh poet and priest, R. S. Thomas, whose many writings wrestled painfully with finding true encounter with our Maker.

The image of the caged tiger is brilliantly employed. So deftly drawn, "up and down in the shadow of its own bulk it went," that at once we can conjure long dimmed memories of the cat house at the zoo—the smell, the fear of lurking danger.

His haunting opening line sets the tone of the entire poem. "It was as beautiful as God must be beautiful. . . .": the pity of this beautiful wild beast put behind bars. And as a result, the onlooker has proximity but no real connection: "the crumpled flower of its face looks into my own, without seeing me."

He hints at an arrest, nearly lifeless, "like moonlight on snow . . . yet breathing. . . ."

Now the unfolding message of the poem: "as you can imagine God breathes within the confines of our definition of him." We have constrained our God behind bars, ripped him away from his true wild habitat, so as to have him near us—in the zoo of our construction.

Result: a mockery of God, an unseeing God, who is only full of regret at the pity of it all, "agonising over immensities that will not return." If we strive to know God, to cage him, instead of allowing him to come and find us, our knowledge will be elusive, "as quiet as moonlight" and as dead.

the White Tiger

It was as beautiful as God
must be beautiful; glacial
eyes that had looked on
violence and come to terms

with it; a body too huge
and majestic for the cage in which
it had been put; up
and down in the shadow

of its own bulk it went,
lifting, as it turned,
the crumpled flower of its face
to look into my own

face without seeing me. It
was the colour of moonlight
on snow and as quiet
as moonlight, but breathing

as you can imagine that
God breathes within the confines
of our definition of him, agonising
over immensities that will not return.

R. S. THOMAS

miracles

Miracles are often misunderstood. We think of them as something to stop us in our tracks, something out of the ordinary, against nature. Whereas it is just the opposite. Miracles are the wonder of all that is commonplace. This human body of mine, these hands that serve me so neatly, my ears, my eyes—the heart that pumps so patiently without complaint, enabling the whole marvelous machine to work so smoothly.

Then to wonder at the size of the stage God has set for me to tread. Did I really need this amazing expanse of exploding universe whose vaste extent and countless miracles causes men to spend their entire lives contemplating outer space? No, but it's a nice generosity!

Some of Christ's miracles were about curing blindness. And I think this is just what they are about, opening our eyes to reality. The miracle of other people, taking them seriously. Remember the man born blind: when he is cured he exclaims, "I see men like trees walking." That is to see things from a fresh angle, using my eyes for the first time to see straight.

And it doesn't require any miracles. That is to say, they are all around me, if only I use my eyes. Open them to reality, again and again. Each fresh day, as the miracle of the dawn chorus opens my ears once more to wonder at the marvel of it all.

miracles

Why
are we shy
of miracles
when we are encircled
by them
all the while

Each morning
is a miracle
as sunrise
wakens me
to my new day
to share with you

Each breath I draw
is a miracle
bringing fresh life
into my lungs

Each thought
each word
each heartbeat
miracles
made mine

Life is full
of miracles
let's own them
use them
to share
and rejoice

JOHN SKINNER
June 2002

masks of God

I remember being haunted by the masks of Venice. You see them in the windows of gift shops. White porcelain, empty eye sockets peering out vacantly from smooth-rounded white cheeks. You are tempted to buy one to hang on the wall back home. But then move on to other distractions; it is not yet Carnival time.

We mask ourself from God in so many clever, varied ways. By running away, flight, putting a clean pair of heels between us and him—which we never can. But we can still try. Or by disguising our actions from ourselves, wearing the mask of this chosen persona, immersing ourself in a role. Or by simple denial. As the boy said of the broken window, "I wasn't there when it happened." Dissociation, the ancient old vanishing trick.

None of which works.

And what are God's masks. Because he employs them too. But somewhat differently. Julian speaks of God's courtesy, the gentle way he approaches us. Almost like catching a horse, gaining our confidence, walking up ever so slowly, lest we shy away.

We use a fragile metaphor to name God's complete otherness, his Majesty—the impossibility of caging the White Tiger. For the truth is he always approaches us, not we him. We must simply wait.

And he comes in many disguises wearing many skillfully fashioned masks, covering his Love. Silently, yet eloquently. Painfully, yet full of loving care for us. And these masks are the camouflage of courtesy. As Christ assured those runaways to Emmaus, "Should not these things have been so?" This is the only way we may meet. To drop my masks and try to watch out for his.

masks of God

The masks of my making
are many

Flight and fear
of being found
by you

Empty business
of my own choosing
to distract from you

Noise and laughter
to fill the emptiness
left by you

And you too have many masks
which shield your face
in courtesy

A mask of majesty
making you unseen

A mask of Silence
where I may listen to your Word

A mask of suffering
where I may share your ways
attending your Mystery
Son of Man
with us
all our ways

JOHN SKINNER
June 2002

The last discourse, those haunting penultimate chapters in John's Gospel—three in all, Jesus' emotionally laden farewell and final message to his friends. But he is also spelling out his love for all of us, how he has generously provided, foreseeing all our needs, now and in the future.

He speaks of going ahead to our eternal home, making up a room for us, our own room, in his Father's house. So the future is secured, have no fear. But what of now, what is to become of us without him?

That too is all in hand. "Keep my word and we will return, my Father and I, and stay with you." So here is a twofold promise: the future is all booked, that's all taken care of, and if we do our bit, remain faithful, leave the door ajar, we will never be alone.

I say all prayer is Trinitarian. This is what Christ's word means. His Father gives him to us in the Silence of our heart. It is for us to receive his gift, the Silence of the Word now made our flesh. And from this gift comes our only possible response, gratitude, and love: the breathing in and out of the Word. Silently knowing that we have visitors.

"We do not know how to pray. But the Spirit within does."

making space

Keep a quiet heart
always trust in God
trust me

There is space for you all
in my Father's house
if there were not
I would never tell you so

I am going now
to prepare your room
And when I am gone
and have made your place
I will return
to take you with me

Then you will be
where I am

You know the way
to the place
where we
are
going

JOHN SKINNER
(based on John 14:1–4)

July

July

Sound deep

Time perhaps to listen to some masters. First, George Fox.

People have sometimes asked me, what is the difference between *Hear our Silence* and the Friends, or Quakers, as outsiders affectionately name them. My reply is—very little—we both know the importance of listening to the Silence. Strangely, only today, I came across an ancient Rosicrucian tradition of Christ's prayer as "entering the Silence" or going on to a mountain or escaping into the desert.

Although Fox frequently preached on hillsides—his first utterance was on a lonely fell to the Seekers, a group of like-minded non-Conformists—the mountain he is referring to is the inner hill of the human heart. So, to paraphrase, be grounded in your own silent prayer and sound the silence of God's presence in everyone. Some bidding, a challenge to live up to.

For we all respect the mountaineer as an athlete who sets himself a tough task and who, if he is to achieve his goal of the summit, will have to watch his step all the way up, as well as caring for every member of his team as if it were he himself. We are all, in a sense, roped for this climb of a lifetime. We don't speak much about it, but just notice the trials and hardships that befall your friends, your family. We put on a brave face most of the time, but the going can be tough and often is.

But that is where tapping into our inner strength and finding the gift of peace within is so vital to our climb and eventual success. Christ spoke of our faith being able to move mountains; our faith will get us to the top, roped alongside all who travel with us.

Sound deep

Keep your feet upon the top
of the mountain

and sound deep
to that of God
in everyone

Mountains are tough to climb
like life
but the view from the top
is awesome

Mountain tops
are for praying
staying
where we find ourselves
in peace

Deep inside
ourselves
within us all

if we listen
we will hear
his Word

Keep your feet upon the top
of the mountain

and sound deep
to that of God
in everyone

GEORGE FOX
(preaching to the Seekers)

A second expert, Rowan Williams, speaks of prayer: simply describing the essence of praying. And he seems to sum up much that we have learned over this year.

> That prayer is not a normal human activity, but a natural response to life, like our very breathing.
>
> That prayer is our attending to our Maker and all that he would give us.
>
> That prayer is finding our real self, not bolstering our false ego.
>
> That prayer is relationship, an unfolding process of Love, initiated by the Other.
>
> That we may not bottle or cage God: or we lose this loving relationship.
>
> That prayer is open-ended, a risk yet also play.
>
> That prayer is never the same, from one moment to the next.
>
> That prayer takes place in the now, not of our choosing.
>
> That prayer is never done, our destination never arrived at.
>
> That we continue to travel each day, if needs be, through the night.
>
> That we are never alone in our praying, for the Spirit of Love surrounds us.

held within his Hands

There comes a time with prayer
when it is no longer
are you seeing something
but
are you being seen

Just as if you are sitting in the Light
just being
and becoming
who you really are

Gathering in awareness

all those sense tentacles
that wriggle outwards
to lay hold of the world
quietly draw them back
into the heart

So that you simply become
what we are
his creature
held within
his Hands

ROWAN WILLIAMS

kneeling

More Thomas, a Welshman, poet, and priest.

Lyrical, real, and above all honest. Again we recognize the hallmarks of someone who has prayed. "Here where prayer has been valid," the self-authenticating tell-tales of true Silent seeking.

I feel he has knelt before his altar, alone, many, many times. And, like Julian, he has frequently come away empty handed—yet calm in the "beseeking." It is not what it seems but what it is. "Waiting for God to speak"? Not quite so literal as that, for Thomas immediately loads in a metaphor that is as diaphanous as it is descriptive.

"The air a staircase for Silence," not much weight-bearing possibilities there, and notice there are no words. We do not ascend these stairs: we wait at the bottom in hope.

"Prompt me God . . . but not yet" . . . as if to say, there must be some vital cipher to utter, yet this is not the time. Later perhaps? And he recognizes that even if God were to utter through these praying lips, something vital would be lost.

"The meaning is in the waiting. . . ." The Silence says it all.

kneeling

Moments of great calm
Kneeling before an altar
of wood in a stone church
in summer

Waiting for the God
to speak

The air a staircase
for Silence

The sun's light
ringing me
as though I acted
a great rôle

And the audiences
still
all that close throng of spirits
waiting
as I
for the message

Prompt me God
But not yet
When I speak
though it be you who speak
through me
something is lost

The meaning
is in the waiting

R. S. THOMAS

the Cloud of Unknowing

This great spiritual classic of the Middle Ages bears no author's name. But circumstantial evidence points to it having been written (and certainly copied) at the Yorkshire Charterhouse of Mount Grace. One expert of early English detects an East Midlands accent (spelling is still fluid now), which would place it once again in the Carthusians' court, another Carthusian Charterhouse being at Leicester. And the whole genre is that of a novice master instructing his young monks in their most important prayer task, the prayer of Silence. If they cannot stay on this ladder, they won't last long.

The title offers us an overriding metaphor for mystical prayer coined by the master author, that of unknowing; our complete powerlessness when we come to prayer. "If you wish to enter this cloud, to be at home in it. . . ." at once I have associations with the mountaineer, heading for the summit, then the clouds gather in. Risky exercise this . . . but the motivation carries us on. We know it's worth our while, more, worth all we can give.

And here also comes John of the Cross with his *nada,* "you must fashion a cloud of forgetting, beneath you and every created thing." Don't let mere things stand in your way. Go lightweight on this mountainside or you will soon tire.

And here also another familiar ring: "the cloud of unknowing will perhaps leave you with the feeling that you are perhaps far from God." Now an immediate and confident reassurance (these mountain guides know their stuff):

"but no, only the absence of the cloud of forgetting keeps you from him now."

Masters all speak the same; they are firm, they are sure, they want us to succeed—or at least to persevere. We are here for one thing, and one thing alone, to listen to the Silence. Forget all else. . . .

The Cloud of Unknowing

If you wish to enter into this cloud
to be at home in it
and to take up the contemplative work of Love
as I urge you
this is what you must do

You must fashion
a cloud of forgetting
beneath you and every created thing

The cloud of unknowing
will perhaps leave you with the feeling
that perhaps you are far from God

But no
only the absence of a cloud of forgetting
keeps you from him now

You are to concern yourself
with no creature
whether material or spiritual

In brief
you must abandon them all
beneath the cloud of forgetting

A CARTHUSIAN?
The Cloud of Unknowing
(Anonymous)

August

August

in our own Image

When I was a Jesuit novice, learning the discipline of silence for most of our day, there came the shock of being bidden to preach my first sermon in the refectory—the rest of the community spread out ten feet below, stuffing their mouths and fastening upon every word I uttered.

We were given but a few tips. The one that sticks is "Don't think you've got to begin in the garden of Eden and work through . . . ." Jesuit humor, or realism pared down.

But, like it or not, our story (and many other similar creation myths) do begin at the beginning. And the Judaeo-Christian myth is specific on one point ("I saw God in a point"), God made us in our own image. That is:

"God said, Let us make man in our own image. . . ."

What blissful storytelling, as Julian might have said. God talks to himself, ruminates alone, and decides: there's only one thing for it. To make mankind: stay for the crunchline—"in our own image."

But he may do none other. Since God is pure love, his actions leave his fingerprints loud and clear upon his work. All he can give is an *imago* of himself. He cannot toss off an inferior work of creation. It must be this one, centered upon Man, the Son of Man, his only Son.

I saw God in a point.

I saw the point of God's working.

I see Christ at the center of our circle, a circle first spelled out five thousand years ago, and again now, in the story we call Genesis, Becoming, how God begat the world. Our memory of our first awakening, wrapped in myth, stories told over and over again in response to so many questions going begging.

"In my end is my beginning. . . ." These questions I must ask. This Silence I must seek. No answers in the back of my *Shilling Arithmetic* book this term (the teacher's got his own copy). All I can do is sit and wait and see. All shall be well, . . . even if it all started a little before my time.

My time is now. Let me use it. And indeed, it is all very good.

"Father, we thank you, . . . that you held these things from the wise, yet revealed them to kids like us."

in our own Image

God said
Let us make man
in our own image
in the likeness of ourselves
and let them be masters
of the fish of the sea
the birds of the heaven
the cattle
and all the wild beasts
and all the reptiles
that crawl upon the earth

God created man
in the image of himself

In the image of God
he created him
male and female
he created
them

And so it was

God
saw all
that he had made
and
indeed
it was
very good

GENESIS 1:26–27, 31

113

Patrick is quite a hero of mine. Must be that Irish grandfather on my mother's side, who (her account), never kept the Faith. Whatever that may mean.

But I'm also sweet on Padraig for his amazing *Confession,* a work of polemical vigo—the equivalent of Botham at his boisterous best. He wrote it from Ireland defending himself against the English bishops who were ganging up on him. Out of jealousy, one supposes, or perhaps because they simply thought he shouldn't be where he was. He was preaching Christ's love "at the ends of the earth." Ireland was quite simply "beyond the pail," as they've tried to tell us ever since.

So Bishop Padraig . . . well let me briefly tell his story. Real *Boy's Own.* Son of a well-to-do father, a romanized English taxman or decurion, also a deacon, his son Patrick was kidnapped by pirates, along with a haul of young men and women, and carted off to Ireland. There he was sold into slavery. The girls into hostile beds, he to care for pigs on a windy hillside. And there he stayed for some seven years.

But there also he learned to pray and consider why this had happened to him.

> I had no option but to surrender myself,
> for I was not yet sixteen years old.
> At that time, I did not recognize the True God:
> that was why I was taken as a captive to Ireland,
> along with many thousands of others with me.
> We fully deserved to suffer like this
> for we had all "turned our back on God";
> we "did not keep his commands."

Came the time, when he knew he had to escape from slavery. And, at risk of life, runaway slaves are always fair targets; he managed a 200-mile traipse along the length of his hostile land, found a boat and made it (via Gaul) back home. But the pull to return soon had him bound to offer himself to be ordained a priest and eventually return as the first messenger of Christ to a people who seemed to need him.

The secret cause of his change, the pull back to the land of his captivity, was love born of prayer. And Patrick tells us how hard he prayed as a prisoner on his hillside.

The Deer's cry, though written long after his death, sums up his spirit.

the Deer's cry

I arise today
in a mighty strength
calling upon the Trinity
believing in the Three Persons
saying they are One
thanking my Creator

I arise today
strengthened by Christ's own baptism
made strong by his crucifixion and his burial
made strong by his resurrection and his ascension
made strong by his descent to meet me on the day of doom

I arise today
with God's strength to pilot me
God's might to uphold me
God's wisdom to guide me
God's eye to look ahead for me
God's ear to hear me
God's word to speak for me
God's hand to defend me
God's way to lie before me
God's shield to protect me

ST. PADRAIG
(traditional)

sack of Self

Try to explain how I came to write this stuff, gather it like strayed wool from a barbed wire fence and attempt to fashion a coat. . . . Impossible.

Words always evaporate, escape upon the page, vanish in the air. Never
trust mere words.
Prefer rather the Silence.
Do I convince you.
Do you dare.
I know I am scared, cowardly, reluctant.
Yet perhaps, and possibly, there may be something in it . . .
We can only try.
Many have gone before . . .
and are still with us . . .
as we also try . . .
in grave and trying times
We know we are not alone.

sack of Self

I close my eyes
and plunge my deaf and groping hand
once more
into this sack of Self

all that I am
is here

The darkness of my making
masks
your
Silent Presence

my deafness mutes
your
Word

Yet as I come
to seek this
Inner Silence
again and again
we dwell together
in safety
at peace
with
my Maker
my Keeper
my Lover

JOHN SKINNER
(for Zez)
July 10, 2002

final words

I let Meister Eckhart have the last say, . . . although there may be many others.

Yet listen to this Master Preacher, teacher, monk and solitary—a man learned enough to become himself, without fear.

All his life, he built communities, his own family of Dominicans, his parish, his scholars: and how? By becoming himself. Fearless, questing, learning, failing, talking, and above all listening.

Master indeed, although he would have not wished that tag. All he did was from deep within, having learned steadily how to receive.

Much of his writings—and he wrote so little, intent as he was upon his preaching—are still the subject of controversy today. He only barely escaped condemnation in his day, trekking to Avignon to answer his case to a somewhat wayward pope. He was accompanied by his brothers, who believed in him.

Today, his call is heard across a wide spectrum of seekers. Searchers after silence, the quench of his words, that echo the Buddha, can this be, no it cannot!

So do we continue to sound the Silence.

God in darkness

Some people

want to find a God

who always shines for them

they may find light

but they mistake it for God

For God shines in the darkness

where often we fail

to recognize him

Where he shines least

is where he shines most

He is in the smallest

as in the greatest

MEISTER ECKHART
Final Words

Epilogue

If you come to this story for the first time, welcome.

If you wish to stay with all this book offers you, welcome.

If you want to contact us and learn more about our continuing work, please contact:

John Skinner
Hear our Silence
1 Purzebrooke House
Musbury Road
Axminster
EX13 5JG
England
wordman.net@boltblue.com

Prayer ultimately is love

+ CYRIL

Together with his wife Judith, and with the collaboration of the Carthusians, John conceived a simple invitation for others to join in the prayer of Silence. *Hear our Silence* workshops invite small groups to come together for a day to experience and explore what prayer means to them. House groups follow, and theirs is a widening circle of friends of *Hear our Silence* who receive our monthly prayer readings, together with a personal letter.